Joseph: The Bigger Picture

REBECCA BERRY

S ince Sunday school, I've loved the ... of Joseph. Despite incredible h... unbelievable lows, God was al...

To set the scene, the writer of Genes... of a complicated domestic situation. Jacob's household could boast rifts in relationships going back years: deep-seated hurts, rivalry, favouritism and perhaps bullying. Do any of those things ring true for you? However perfect they might seem, most families will carry their own baggage, insecurity and tension. Why? Because they're made up of imperfect people who didn't necessarily choose each other.

any of his other sons' (v3)

I have two older (twin) sisters, and I'm completely in awe of both: one a cardiac nurse, who I saw in action when she helped nurse my father-in-law in his final days, and the other a primary school teacher with the sweetest and funniest dinnertime stories I've ever heard. Even though my parents have no favourites, I've always considered my sisters to be two very hard acts to follow, and even spent some years convinced that I didn't deserve for my parents to be proud of me too.

However, as the golden boy, Joseph was actively hated – his father's love for him only caused division and derision. Yes, he was cocky and spoilt, and to think we're better than other people is arrogant and dangerous. But the belief that we're unworthy, unseen and unqualified can be every bit as damaging, and only holds us back.

You already have something in common with Joseph: you are recklessly, extravagantly and fiercely loved and adored by your Father. Only He has no favourites, and nothing bad can come from His love for you.

Weekend

Not yet

....

For reflection: Genesis 37:5–11

'And they hated him all the more because of his dream and what he had said.' (v8)

Even though Joseph was undoubtedly hearing from God, I find it quite hard to find anyone behaving particularly brilliantly in today's verses. Young and enthusiastic, Joseph totally jumped the gun, blurting out his vision without a scrap of humility. And it didn't go down well.

Though he had an incredible destiny ahead of him, Joseph simply wasn't ready yet. If God had taken an arrogant teenager and immediately made him prime minister, we'd be reading a very different story. It would be another 13 years (thereabouts) before Joseph was the man he needed to be.

If you know that God has something in store for you but it just hasn't happened yet, be encouraged – either He is still working on you, or working on the circumstances around you. 1 Peter 5:6–7 in *The Message* says this: 'So be content with who you are, and don't put on airs. God's strong hand is on you; he'll promote you at the right time. Live carefree before God; he is most careful with you.' I've heard it said that God has two speeds: slowly, and suddenly. Mostly it's the former... but His timing is always perfect.

....

Optional further reflection

Read 2 Peter 3:9 (especially in *The Message*) and consider God's big picture plans for the world. How do these verses speak personally to you today?

Inspiring
Women
Every Day

November

JOSEPH: THE
BIGGER PICTURE

REBECCA BERRY

December

NO GREATER LOVE

LYN GITCHEL

Plus... 'Be Inspired' article, CWR Today pages
and CWR Ministry Events

MIX
Paper from
responsible sources
FSC® C015900
www.fsc.org

Rebecca Berry

Rebecca Berry is Lead Editor at CWR, but secretly her first love is writing (she just doesn't do much of it). She loves working on anything that helps people to understand more about the Bible, God and themselves. Rebecca lives in Surrey with her husband Chris, but a tiny piece of her heart will always belong to Suffolk.

Lyn Gitchel

Lyn Gitchel was born and educated in England, but is now based in North Carolina. She was ordained in 1964 and worked with CWR for several years before meeting her husband and moving to the US, where they pastored churches together until his death in 1997. Lyn has authored a number of Bible study books, available on Amazon.

Copyright © CWR 2019. Published by CWR, Waverley Abbey House, Waverley Lane, Farnham, Surrey GU9 8EP, UK. Tel: 01252 784700 Email: mail@cwr.org.uk
Registered Charity No. 294387. Registered Limited Company No. 1990308.
Front cover image: Stocksy/Ani Dimi
Concept development, editing, design and production by CWR. Printed in England by Linney.

Betrayal

Genesis 37:12–27

> "'Here comes that dreamer!' they said to each other. "Come now, let's kill him'" (vv19–20)

The Bible doesn't often present us with clean-cut 'good guys' and 'bad guys' (Jesus being the obvious exception). Everyone written about was human, and everyone was flawed. But even if we don't particularly like Joseph at the beginning of his story, most of us would agree that his 'punishment' (slavery, downgraded at the last minute from death) doesn't exactly fit his 'crime' (being a little bit arrogant and spoilt). Joseph might have needed knocking down a peg or two, but being sold into slavery by his older brothers, the very people who should have loved and protected him the most, is one of the worst betrayals imaginable – a betrayal known by Jesus, sold out by one of His closest friends. Utterly hated, rejected, heartbroken and terrified, Joseph had no idea that this moment of betrayal would actually shift the trajectory of his life towards everything he had dreamed of.

We all know what it is to be let down, or to experience a feeling of hopelessness to some degree. But to believe that God often does His best work at rock-bottom takes a level of faith that sometimes only comes to us in retrospect. When things seem broken beyond our comprehension, it's hard to imagine how things could possibly look different.

Without opening up past hurts that you've already dealt with, think about the lowest point in your own life and ask God to show you where He was at work. Did you feel closer to Him, or further away? And if you're currently at a point in your life where you're struggling to understand what God could possibly be doing, trust that He can turn things around.

For prayer and reflection

Jesus, You know what it is to be let down. Help me to know You closely today, whatever I face. Amen.

Not the end of the story

**Genesis
37:28–36;
Matthew 27:1–5**

'When Reuben
returned to the
cistern and saw
that Joseph was
not there, he
tore his clothes.'
(Gen. 37:29)

As if selling their brother into slavery wasn't bad enough, the brothers sank even lower to the point of letting their beloved father believe that Joseph had been torn to pieces by a wild animal. Now Joseph wasn't the only victim of this betrayal: it nearly destroyed Jacob and, ironically, the brothers themselves, who ended up trapping themselves in a conspiracy that they would have to maintain – a lie that would imprison them in their own guilt and shame for years to come.

Jealousy and fear can lead to unthinkable acts against others, and betrayal will hurt even the betrayer. Reuben tore his clothes – perhaps in despair, annoyance or shame – but he was able to go home with a pocketful of change and live, however painfully, with what he'd done. The same can't be said of Judas Iscariot who, having handed over Jesus to be crucified, felt unable to keep his money or his life. I think it's one of the biggest tragedies of the Bible that, unlike Joseph's brothers, Judas didn't live to be reconciled with the one he'd betrayed. He never got to see how God was powerful enough to use his betrayal to trigger the most incredible act of redemption in history. Joseph's brothers thought that betrayal was the end of the story; they were wrong. Judas thought that betrayal was the end of the story; he was wrong.

Whatever we've done, there's nothing God can't use. A friend of mine recently reposted something on social media, and it really stuck with me: 'If you think you've blown God's plan for your life, rest in this: you, my beautiful friend, are not that powerful.'

*Quote widely attributed to Lisa Bever

**For prayer
and reflection**

Lord Jesus, when I
think it's the end of
the story, help me
to remember Your
redemptive power.
Thank You for
loving me in all my
fallibility. Amen.

CWR Ministry Events

Please pray for the team

DATE	EVENT	PLACE	PRESENTER(S)
2 Nov	Insight into Anxiety and Depression	Lifecentral Church, Birmingham	Mick Brooks and team
6 Nov	Sharing Your Faith – Naturally	Waverley Abbey House	Andy Peck
7 Nov	What Does Healthy Church Growth Look Like?	WAH	Andy Peck
9 Nov	Waverley Abbey College Open Day	WAH	WAC team
13 Nov	Energising Your Small Group	WAH	Andy Peck
14 Nov	Renewing Your Mind	WAH	Andy Peck
15 Nov	Healthy You, Healthy School	WAH	Derek Holbird and guests
20 Nov	Structuring Pastoral Care	WAH	Andy Peck
27 Nov	Great Chapters of the Bible	WAH	Philip Greenslade
28 Nov	Practising the Presence of God	WAH	Andy Peck
4 Dec	Inspiring Women Christmas Celebration	WAH	Angie Green and the Inspiring Women team
5 Dec	Advent Supper	WAH	Philip Greenslade

Please pray for our students and tutors on our ongoing BA Counselling programme at Waverley Abbey College (which takes place at Waverley Abbey House), as well as our Certificate in Christian Counselling and MA Counselling qualifications.

We would also appreciate prayer for our ongoing ministry in Singapore and Cambodia, as well as the many regional events that will be happening around the UK this year.

For further information and a full list of CWR's courses, seminars and events, call **(+44) 01252 784719** or visit **cwr.org.uk/courses**

You can also download our free Prayer Track, which includes daily prayers, from **cwr.org.uk/prayertrack**

Right where we are

Genesis 39:1–6

'When his master saw that the LORD was with him and that the LORD gave him success in everything he did, Joseph found favour in his eyes' (vv3–4)

Being both a millennial and a job-hunting graduate during a recession was a huge learning curve for me. I took a waitressing job in my hometown, but although it was a 'very nice establishment', the owner was notoriously difficult, and it wasn't at all what I wanted to be doing. You could say I empathised with Joseph: having believed I was special, I was surprised to find myself as a servant (of sorts), working strange hours on minimum wage. But my sense of entitlement took a well-needed beating, and I decided to roll up my sleeves. I befriended all the regulars and learned the 52-bottle wine list from memory. Years later, I can honestly say that it was invaluable experience, and I am who I am because of that job. I don't know how, but I found a way to work with the boss, and we eventually parted ways with a handshake, not a slamming door.

Joseph never aspired to be a slave, but when he became one, he became the best slave there was. It helped that he landed on his feet in a good household with a good master, but his integrity spoke volumes. After some serious ego realignment, his character turned heads. Why? Because 'the LORD was with Joseph'. We read that repeatedly. The Lord was with Joseph as he worked his fingers to the bone – and the Lord was with Rebecca Berry when she held her own behind that bar and turfed out the eccentric local inebriates at closing time.

They say that the only really safe place to be is right where God wants you. Jesus' name is Immanuel – God with us. He is *with us*. Whatever your situation, you carry God's presence with you today. Make the most of it.

For prayer and reflection

Immanuel, thank You for the immovable truth that You are with me. Stay close to me today. Amen.

Doing **the right thing**

Genesis 39:6–23

'How then could I do such a wicked thing and sin against God?' (v9)

I f we're looking for evidence of Joseph's integrity, maturity and courage, today's passage is a good place to start. He is young, 'well-built and handsome' (v6), and the boss's wife is offering herself to him on a silver platter – but Joseph knows that to take what isn't his would dishonour both his God and his master. Somehow he has the strength to get out of there, but doing the right thing only lands him in more trouble. Even if Potiphar had his suspicions about his wife's behaviour (we only read that he 'burned with anger' – we don't know towards whom), there's no way he could take the word of a slave over hers. So Joseph is left in prison to discover a whole new rock-bottom.

Perhaps you know what it is to do the right thing, only to end up somehow persecuted for it and wondering if God has totally forsaken you. If there's one thing we learn from Joseph's story, it's this: He hasn't. But I'm also wondering if we can identify with Mrs Potiphar here a little bit too. Have you ever expected to get your own way, but seen things backfire horribly? Have you ever had your pride hurt, and lashed out as a result? If I'm honest, there have been times where I've pointed the finger at others to get myself out of a mess of my own making. No one's gone to prison as a result, but I've done it.

We're all capable of being manipulative when we're in danger of being exposed, but never underestimate the value of integrity. If it's Mrs Potiphar you identify with today, ask God to gently convict you, forgive you and show you how to put things right. If you identify more with Joseph, hang in there.

For prayer and reflection

Pray for those who are unjustly imprisoned. Pray for courage, comfort and ultimately, justice.

Dreams **reawakened**

Genesis 40:1–8

'Then Joseph said to them, "Do not interpretations belong to God? Tell me your dreams."' (v8)

Though he has established his character, proven his integrity and prospered under less than perfect conditions, Joseph once again finds himself stripped of everything he has, and thrown in prison on false charges of sexual assault. Surely it can't get any worse.

But here we see that Joseph has learned humility. Despite gaining the respect of the warden and being granted favour and responsibility, Joseph isn't leading a prison gang or abusing what little authority he has. Instead, he shows compassion for the suffering of his fellow inmates: 'he saw that they were dejected' (v6) and offers his sympathy and assistance.

What had become of Joseph's dreams while in Egypt? We don't know. After the shock and trauma of being sold into slavery, did he continue to hear from God in the quiet of the night, or had his gift for dreaming been dormant all that time? Did he sleep much at all in prison, and if so, was he plagued by nightmares?

Whatever the answer, this is a key moment – but he is no longer the cocky teenager, desperate for the respect and affirmation of his brothers. Instead of taking any credit for himself, all glory goes to God (v8). This is the first time Joseph speaks of his faith in God, but it is a bold statement of his awareness that He is with him.

When it comes to exercising our gifts, courage and confidence are important – but so is humility. When we acknowledge where our skill, creativity and talent comes from, we are far more likely to use it *for* God. Do you have gifts that are 'dormant' right now? Ask God for an opportunity to reawaken them.

For prayer and reflection

Father God, thank You for the gifts You have given me. Help me to step out in using them for Your enjoyment as well as my own. Amen.

Remember me

....

For reflection: Genesis 40:9–15

'remember me and show me kindness; mention me to Pharaoh and get me out of this prison' (v14)

With the interpretation of his inmates' dreams comes some good news and some bad news. The good news: Pharaoh's former barman will soon be released from prison and get his job back! The sun is coming out. (The bad news: it won't be such a bright forecast for the baker.) Joseph has just one request: 'when all goes well with you, remember me and show me kindness; mention me to Pharaoh' (v14).

We all want to be known, valued and remembered. If we've done someone a service, it's nice to be acknowledged and thanked (though we're told to serve others even without recognition or appreciation). Being forgotten or overlooked can be incredibly hurtful. If you have wounds in this area, ask God for His encouragement and healing. He has not forgotten you. It is against His nature to forget you. He won't *ever* forget you.

The barman would soon be in a position to speak up for Joseph, but he would forget him. This Sunday, we remember those who fought for our freedom, and respond to their request that we don't forget them. Who needs us to fight (or speak up) for them today?

....

Optional further reading

Ephesians 1:7–10

Lest we **forget**

**Genesis
40:14–23**

'The chief
cupbearer,
however, did not
remember Joseph;
he forgot him.'
(v23)

Marking 101 years since the armistice of the First World War, today is a timely reminder of the dangers of forgetting. We are free, but that freedom has been paid for with the lives of others – and ultimately with the sacrifice of One.

I love that today's Bible reading mentions it was Pharaoh's birthday. Clearly he felt that an appropriate way to celebrate would be to reinstate one prisoner and have the other one executed. (If he had reinstated the baker instead, perhaps he might have had a cake.) I can't help but wonder if the barman truly forgot about Joseph, or if he just 'forgot' him – it was his first day back on the job, and it was a pretty serious gig. Maybe he was scared to risk it all on account of a prisoner Pharaoh had probably never heard of. Or perhaps he really was just so busy living the good life that he was swift to blot out that dark chapter of incarceration. Either way, 'he forgot him'.

As if being rejected by his brothers wasn't the low point, Joseph had been sold into slavery, wrongfully accused of sexual assault, sacked and imprisoned, and now forgotten. And the barman's neglect would cost Joseph another two years of freedom.

Sometimes we can forget something out of convenience, simply because it's too hard for us to comprehend or too uncomfortable to think about. Without having lived through the reality of war, it can be difficult to grasp the sacrifice of countless soldiers. How often do you allow yourself to remember what Jesus has saved you from, and what it cost Him to do so? Approach your life with liberty today, and say thank you.

**For prayer
and reflection**

Ask God to help
you remember
someone you might
have forgotten.
Remember them;
thank them; honour
them.

No one could

After two long years, the penny finally dropped for Pharaoh's barman, and the day came when Joseph would see breakthrough. Pharaoh was being kept up at night searching for answers to questions he didn't even understand. Despite having every resource in the kingdom at his disposal to help him, 'no one could'. God afflicted him with a restlessness he couldn't ignore, but He also provided him with the solution, neatly packaged in the form of Joseph, safely under lock and key.

All around us, people are searching for answers everywhere and anywhere, but nothing satisfies. Perhaps you (or those you know) have experienced what it is to have every box in life ticked but still feel empty. There's no authority to be found in vague spirituality and 'positive vibes'. As the saying goes, fine words butter no parsnips – and Pharaoh knew that. He wasn't going to settle for the answer he liked best, but the truth. And so in a single verse, Joseph is summoned, shaved, showered, given a haircut and some new threads, and presented to the royal court. Showtime.

Joseph's reputation may have preceded him, but the first words out of his mouth sum up everything he now knows to be true: 'I cannot do it… but God can.' Just as when he listened to the dreams of his fellow prisoners, all the credit goes to the one who gave him the gift in the first place. He understands that only God has the answers. Having been stripped of everything else in the last 13 years, Joseph knows he can count on the goodness, capability and endless possibility of the God he serves.

Genesis 41:8–24

'Pharaoh told them his dreams, but no one could interpret them for him.' (v8)

For prayer and reflection

Father, 'whatever were gains to me I now consider loss for the sake of Christ' (Phil. 3:7). Thank You for the incredible joy of knowing You. Amen.

In on **the plan**

Genesis
41:25–45

'God has revealed
to Pharaoh what
he is about to do.'
(v25)

Thirteen years of character building, ego realignment and overcoming challenges had made Joseph a humble and patient man of integrity. He had learnt to trust wholly in God and use the gifts that He had given him, all for His glory. He'd been able to practise his gift with his two fellow prisoners and build his confidence in his God-given abilities so that by this point, he is able to hear from God so clearly that he doesn't even stutter.

God is mysterious; He is vast; He is all-powerful; He is far too huge for our tiny human minds to fully comprehend. But that doesn't mean He is absent, silent or indifferent. Though He is the master of the universe, God does not withhold Himself from us. Presumably, Pharaoh wasn't actively seeking God – he was probably reigning as he saw fit, and happily worshipping a variety of mythical gods and statues. Yet God gave the dreams of the corn and the cows directly to him. He allowed Pharaoh to be in on the plan. If we ever think that praying for world leaders and politicians is a waste of time, today's reading offers a pretty compelling argument for the contrary. God can speak to anyone.

Joseph's words to Pharaoh are so precise that no one in the royal court can refute the presence of the God in Joseph (vv38–39). Arguably, that's what gets him promoted. The results are so incredible that royalty has to sit up and pay attention. Pharaoh isn't about to let power like this simply leave the building.

However small and insignificant you might feel, God has chosen to make His home in you. The same Spirit of God that worked in Joseph works in you too. You are in on the plan.

For prayer
and reflection

**God, though I
will never fully
understand Your
ways, thank You
for making me a
part of Your plans.
Help me to seek
You, even when
I think You are
silent. Amen.**

Journey to Christmas

Despite centuries of prophecies, all revealing a divine plan for humanity written in eternity, Jesus' coming to earth as a vulnerable baby was – to those who waited for Him – totally unexpected.

Though it's a story many of us read year upon year at Christmastime, enjoy a change of pace this Advent as the team from the 24-7 Prayer movement guide you through 31 days of Bible reading, prayer and liturgical reflection. Beginning on Advent Sunday, journey with Elizabeth and Zachariah, Mary and Joseph as you P.R.A.Y. your way through December:

- Pause – remove all distractions, be still and make room to connect with God
- Rejoice and Reflect – give thanks, before engaging with a short passage of Scripture
- Ask – bring your questions to God
- Yield – surrender to God's will for your life

As a contemporary take on an ancient practice, the prayers written have been inspired by Christian heroes and traditions throughout the centuries and designed to be returned to daily, making space for *selah* (opportunities to pause, wait and respond).

Group discussion notes are also included, should you want to go on this Advent journey with others.

Journey to Christmas is written by Pete Greig, Carla Harding, Phil Togwell and Jill Weber at 24-7 Prayer.

Order now in time for Advent.
For price and purchasing information,
visit cwr.org.uk/shop

Just **getting started**

**Genesis
41:46–52**

'Joseph was thirty
years old when he
entered the service
of Pharaoh king of
Egypt.' (v46)

Today is my thirtieth birthday.

If I am to measure the 'success' of my life so far in comparison to Joseph's, then it's a mixed bag. I've never been to prison (unless something has gone spectacularly wrong since these notes went to print); on the other hand, I'm not exactly the prime minster of anywhere either. But I can say that there isn't room on this page to list all the things I am thankful for, and all that I am still excited for.

My journey from age 17 to age 30 hasn't been marred by betrayal and persecution, but it hasn't gone exactly the way I originally planned. And I have to say I'm incredibly relieved. If I'd neatly progressed from one significant life event to the next in tidy intervals of two years at a time, I might have drifted into a coma. The most fun I've had so far, and the closest I've been to God along the way, has been when my tidy plans and expectations have gone out of the window. I'm now where I very much believe I'm meant to be, only having taken a route far more interesting than the one I would have planned for myself.

I wonder if there was a specific moment when Joseph looked back on everything he'd been through to get to this point, flooded with the astounding revelation that maybe, just maybe, God really did have a plan all along. Maybe he was so dumbfounded by the speed at which it was happening that he thought he was back in dreamland.

Joseph was 30 when things started getting interesting; Mary was 14; Moses was 80. However old you are today, I hope God fills you with fresh excitement and anticipation for what He is still yet to do in your life.

**For prayer
and reflection**

**Spend some time
thinking about
significant
moments or
seasons in your
life so far, whether
positive or
negative, when
you were most
excited about what
God was doing.**

Pride and prejudice

Genesis 42:1–17

'Although Joseph recognised his brothers, they did not recognise him.' (v8)

And so we are brought to the moment when Joseph is face to face with the men who sold him out – or, more to the point, they are face-down on the ground, exactly as he had dreamed all those years before. It's a bizarre and unexpected situation, and Joseph's abrupt and defensive stance is most likely a self-preservation tactic. The safest place for him to hide is behind his disguise.

But maybe there's more to it than that. As well as the shock, bitterness or anger that he might have been trying to suppress, I wonder if the overriding feeling here is pride. Joseph had always known he was someone special and, back in the same room as his brothers, perhaps the teenager in him has resurfaced. Only they don't even know it's him! Even now, they are still unable to see how special he is. Ouch.

Remember that Joseph is effectively the prime minister at this point and is still following God, aware that He has made things work for good. But something holds him back in this first meeting. Interestingly, the brothers identify themselves as being of 'twelve brothers... and one is no more' (v13). Whether maintaining their lie or just having given up on there being any other explanation, Joseph is dead to them. Furthermore, they later show a concern for their brother Benjamin, which they couldn't ever muster for Joseph.

If someone has hurt you or your pride badly enough, the thought of forgiving them can seem impossible, overwhelming or even unjust. If there's something stopping you from moving forward, ask for God's strength to keep wrestling with it until it's out of your way.

For prayer and reflection

Father, when my pride is hurt, help me not to react out of how I feel, but to respond knowing who I am in You. Amen.

It takes time

....

For reflection: Genesis 42:18–38

'What is this that God has done to us?' (v28)

According to the Sunday school version of this story, surely we're almost at the big finale: Joseph's running the show, is happily married and settled down, and his brothers have just turned up in Egypt... except we're only halfway through the month. Most of the milestones of Joseph's life – dreams, betrayal, slavery, imprisonment, breakthrough, promotion – are all dealt with in just a few tidy chapters of Genesis. So why does the reconciliation part take so long? Perhaps it's because this story isn't as much about Joseph being dumped in a pit and then doing well out of it as it is about restoring relationships. There is still a lot of healing to take place, and it will take time, effort and patience.

I feel genuinely sorry for the brothers at this point. Like Joseph, they've also been imprisoned (in their case by their own guilt and shame), only they haven't prospered. They are exactly where they were the day they sold their brother.

While guilt can be a healthy indication that we've done wrong, shame attacks who we are and is not from God. Don't let shame hold you back – there is forgiveness, and there is freedom.

....

Optional further reading

John 8:1–11 in *The Passion Translation*
Heather Churchill and Claire Musters, *Insight into Shame*
(Farnham: CWR, 2019)

Testing, testing

Without knowing the true identity of the man in Egypt in charge of all the grain, the brothers must be wondering what on earth is going on. No wonder it brings all their regret to the surface (Gen. 42:28). Terrified that history will repeat itself and they will end up robbing their father of another son, they'll do whatever it takes to avoid making the mistakes of the past. Perhaps Jacob also feels responsible for Joseph's 'death', given that his last words to him were those sending him out to the fields where he was supposedly devoured by a wild animal. The general atmosphere within the family is one of tension and fear.

I love a good murder mystery on TV (fetch me my slippers and a cup of Earl Grey), especially when the sleuthing detective messes with the suspects' minds in order to expose the guilty party – it's fun to watch the potential culprits sweat a bit. But I don't think Joseph is deliberately playing mind games here just to obtain an admission of guilt. In his book *Living the Dream*, Dave Smith suggests that this series of testing is Joseph's way of rebuilding trust. It could be that Joseph has already forgiven his brothers, but wants to be sure that their repentance is genuine, and their reconciliation long-lasting. Further to that, he sends them home with their silver – possibly a nod to the silver they sold him for, but also a clear indication of his concern that they don't starve. No wonder they are scratching their heads.

Betrayed trust can be a very difficult thing to recover, but it is possible. Thankfully, God's grace is not as cautious as we are.

Genesis 43:1–14

'I myself will guarantee his safety; you can hold me personally responsible for him.' (v9)

For prayer and reflection

Jesus, if secure relationships are built on trust, then today, right now, I trust in You. Amen.

**Genesis
43:15–34**

'Deeply moved at
the sight of his
brother, Joseph
hurried out and
looked for a place
to weep.' (v30)

Coming up for **air**

After university, I did a discipleship training programme with Youth With A Mission, which meant six months away from my boyfriend of two years. Though I had the time of my life, I couldn't wait for the day when I'd get home and he would pick me up from the airport.

Typically, I was the last off the plane, and my bag the last off the carousel... but at last I was walking through to Arrivals and caught a glimpse of him through the crowds of waiting people. Even though I had been looking forward to seeing him for so many months, I suddenly felt the wind knocked out of me. So, did I run towards him like the end of a movie? Not exactly. Instead I deliberately steered my luggage trolley behind someone else so that he would once again be temporarily out of sight. I just needed a second to compose myself. It was a mental and emotional coming up for air.

I wonder if Joseph felt something similar when he saw Benjamin. He'd spent years wondering if he'd ever see his father or any of his brothers ever again – perhaps imagining what he'd say to them, or have them say to him. When the day finally came when they were once again in the same room, he needed some space to process all that emotion – just a bit more time to prepare for the reality of getting something he'd hoped for for so long.

I only needed a few seconds to overcome my shyness, get a grip and then run towards the man I'm now married to at Heathrow. Joseph needed a few more signs, as we'll see over the next few days. Life can be full of moments of high emotion. It's OK for us to take our time. Be patient with others. Be patient with yourself.

**For prayer
and reflection**

**Lord, thank You for
being so patient
and gracious
towards me. Help
me to show that
same kindness to
myself and to
others. Amen.**

Brothers

'How can I go back to my father if the boy is not with me?' (v34)

I f you have time to read the whole of Genesis 44 today, it's well worthwhile – scenes of drama, intrigue and testing. As we considered on Monday, Joseph may simply be enjoying watching his brothers squirm, or he could be testing their sincerity and rebuilding trust.

As this reconciliation saga plays out, what's fascinating is the contrast of Joseph and his brother Judah. Twenty years previously, Judah had been the mastermind behind the betrayal plot (Gen. 37:26–27), but through our New Testament lens, we know that he was destined to be a forefather of Jesus (Matt. 1) – so his redemption and transformation here is pretty pivotal for the bigger picture. Despite the obvious flaws of both men, Dave Smith suggests, 'this whole section can be seen as a powerful foreshadowing of the person and work of Jesus. Both Judah, through his offer of intercession and substitution, and Joseph, betrayed and yet granting forgiveness to his brothers, can be seen as "types" of the promised Messiah.' This story signposts Jesus. Even so many years before His incarnation, God is writing a story of redemption and forgiveness, foreshadowed through the narratives of flawed individuals and their seemingly lowest moments.

The heartfelt way in which Judah pleads with Joseph (particularly in vv30–34) indicates his contrition, motivation and resolve to honour his father and his family. Whatever their differences in the past, here are two brothers, flesh and blood, bound by a fierce love for their father. No further proof is required. Judah has passed the test.

*Dave Smith, *Living the Dream* (Farnham: CWR, 2016) p117

For prayer and reflection

Lord Jesus, I thank You that no one is a write-off. You can transform anyone. Help me to remember that and forgive without hesitating. Amen.

Grace

Genesis 45:1–15

'And he kissed all his brothers and wept over them. Afterwards his brothers talked with him.' (v15)

A t long last, after quite the build-up, this is the moment: Joseph shakes off his disguise and reveals his true identity.

It must have been pretty awkward in that room for a few seconds – before Joseph can even speak, he starts sobbing 'so loudly that the Egyptians heard him, and Pharaoh's household heard about it' (v2). Imagine eleven burly guys, all feeling slightly bewildered while the 'lord of all Egypt' (v9) has a full-on emotional meltdown in front of them. And then, supposedly as an explanation, they're thrown a massive curveball: 'Remember that brother you sold into slavery and assumed to be dead? Well, it's me! Surprise!' Their response? They are 'unable to answer him, because they [are] terrified at his presence' (v3). Seems fair.

Despite this being the first time he feels able to speak freely and openly with his brothers with no pretence, Joseph extends nothing but grace upon grace to them. He really could let them have it – he could throw them in jail, make them his slaves or let them starve to death. But instead, his verdict is this: 'do not be distressed and do not be angry with yourselves' (v5); 'God sent me ahead of you' (v7); 'I will provide for you' (v11).

Have you ever wasted time assuming God was furious with you, and ended up becoming furious with yourself, too afraid to sort things out with Him? Have you ever expected punishment and been offered grace instead? When we know we deserve a serious telling-off and are instead met with an embrace and a clean slate, it's a little bit confusing. But that's how our God operates.

For prayer and reflection

Father God, instead of what I deserve, You offer me grace. May the awesome truth of that fact never be lost on me. Amen.

The **best** of all

'the best of all
Egypt will be
yours' (45:20)

My husband and I moved house last summer. Our new house was only a couple of towns away, so we were able to keep the same jobs and remain part of the same church. We'd been crammed into a one-bedroom flat for several years, so slimming down our clutter wasn't too much of a mission, and we don't yet have children – so all we really had to do was get some boxes, borrow a van, and drive the 15-minute journey back and forth a few times. It was hugely exciting and not that complicated; it was also exhausting, terrifying and just about as stressful as we expected.

I can't imagine the mass-scale evacuation operation required to move Jacob and all his descendants from Canaan to Egypt. Even though it meant escaping famine and disaster, it can't have been easy. But in following God's plan and allowing Him to rescue them, there would only be good things in store for Joseph's family – 'the best', in fact (Gen. 45:20).

The first few verses of Genesis 46 tell us a lot about the character of God. He is present and involved, speaking to Jacob personally (v2). He is faithful: 'I am God, the God of your father' (v3). He is comforting: 'Do not be afraid' (v3). He has big plans: 'I will make you into a great nation there' (v3). He is trustworthy: 'I will surely bring you back again' (v4). And He is kind: 'Joseph's own hand will close your eyes' (v4).

Taking the next step, however big or small, can be hugely daunting (unless you're somebody who relishes a challenge and embraces change – in which case, I salute you!). But remember that wherever God is taking you next, He knows what He is doing.

For prayer and reflection

Jesus, I trust You to lead me on this journey. Whatever You have in store for me, help me to be ready to embrace it. Amen.

Karen Case Green

Where art meets faith

Karen lectured at the University of Surrey before training for Baptist ordination. She is actively involved in her church and is a member of the Inspiring Women team here at CWR. She tells us more about her love of looking at faith through a creative lens...

• •

I've walked a 'lilypad' faith. As someone who likes to plan ahead and have certainty, I'd love the path to be laid out clearly, with an obvious destination and an ETA! God has different methods. Moving countries, having children and changing careers have all had me wondering at times why things can't move more directly. Instead, I find that God leads me one lilypad at a time and that the work that happens in the waiting seems as important as reaching the final destination.

But I'm also learning that God really cares about the desires of my heart and wants to lead me into them. I love beauty and creativity, and I saw God as the source of both from an early age when I stumbled across them in the world. However, I couldn't see many examples of either in the gathered church. Sure, there was lots (and lots) of singing, but other forms of creativity? For years, I felt I had to keep my love of the arts separate from my Christian faith. I almost quit studying English at university, feeling embarrassed that it wasn't more 'useful'. (Turns out I'd be rubbish at 'useful'!)

One day I admitted my frustration to my minister. He encouraged me to do an MA at King's College, London in Christianity and the Arts. 'Do it just for the love of it,' he said. It felt quite wasteful, and I wavered. I was a mother of two. I was also juggling a teaching job at the University of Surrey alongside voluntary ministry at church. There wasn't much spare time – or cash.

But with my husband's encouragement, I dropped some things and did the course. It was one of the best decisions I've ever made! As well as teaching me how much the Church valued art in the past, I also woke up to what some are calling a 'new renaissance' – a flourishing in the visual arts and faith today. Suddenly, my yearning for images and stories that presented the world differently wasn't wasteful; it was OK. In fact, it was a longing that God had put inside me!

On my last piece of work, my tutor wrote, 'May what you've done here be really fruitful.' I hung on to those words of promise and walked towards them.

I began to connect with other people who shared this desire for creativity and beauty in the Church. Over coffee one day, one artist suddenly said, 'Why don't we write a course together?' We wanted to look at the salvation story through the lens of the arts, and to encourage people to 'make' in response – through words and visual art. We co-wrote, slowly, as both of us were juggling motherhood and ordination training. We called the course 'Imaging the Story'. We've had so much fun running it, and the book is now finally out. Who'd have known that that one lilypad step, taken years ago, would have landed me here? God hears the desires of our hearts.

Wait
and see what comes
to fill
the gaping hole
in your chest.
Wait with your hands open
to receive what could never come
except to what is empty
and hollow...

Wait for it.
Still yourself.
Stay.

From Jan Richardson, *Circle of Grace: A Blessing for the Seasons* (Orlando, FL: Wanton Godspeller, 2015).

• •

When the wait is over

....

For reflection: Genesis 46:26–47:12

'he threw his arms around his father and wept for a long time'
(46:29)

The last time Joseph had seen his father was the day he'd been sent after his brothers in the fields (Gen. 37:14). We can only imagine what went through the minds of both Jacob and Joseph in these moments, years later, as they walked towards each other. For all that time, Jacob held onto the hope that he would see his son again – even though, if his other sons were to be believed, there was no hope.

Such was his happiness that he said, 'Now I am ready to die' (v30). The final item on the bucket list was ticked. (This is the pass-the-tissues moment, when the violins are playing and the drama is mostly over.)

When the wait is over and our hopes are realised, it's often euphoric, sometimes underwhelming… occasionally disappointing. We don't always get the reunion, the closure or the conclusion that we hope for. Life can get messy, and things aren't always tidily sorted out in the nick of time. Are you mourning a relationship or seeking closure over something? If it seems to be too late, know that God can help you let go. If not, ask for His wisdom as to how you can put things right.

....

Optional further reading

Luke 15:20–24

Endurance

Genesis 47:13–31

'both Egypt and Canaan wasted away because of the famine' (v13)

After all the reuniting and reconciling that's been going on, it's a bit jarring to be reminded of the seven-year famine ravaging Egypt and the surrounding nations. Though Joseph had done a great job of executing God's contingency plan for food storage, there would still be several more years of no harvest. Despite repaired relationships, Joseph's family would have to learn to work as a team in order to survive.

Just over a year ago, my husband was involved in a serious road collision. Though we are enormously grateful that he wasn't killed, paralysed or left brain-dead, he still suffered serious injuries requiring follow-up surgery, and it was a very traumatic time. The recovery process has been long, and we have also had to deal with police, insurance companies and solicitors. We've been hugely supported and blessed, but we've needed that blessing to see us through a season of endurance (and we're still praying it won't last seven years).

Joseph doesn't seem to come off too brilliantly in parts of today's reading, especially when we read that he 'reduced the people to servitude' (v21). But he had evidently developed his political acumen and remained loyal to Pharaoh, while taking care of the best interests of his people (v27). He was clearly the right man for a very difficult job.

The recent global political landscape has made 2019 a fascinating time to be alive. It's so important that we pray for our leaders. Regardless of whether or not we agree with their ideas, they carry the weight of leading us through difficult challenges. Pharaoh heard directly from God, so anybody can. Pray on.

For prayer and reflection

Where do you have influence? Do you wield it justly? Ask God to give you wisdom.

Immeasurably **more**

Genesis 48:1–11

'I never expected to see your face again, and now God has allowed me to see your children too.'
(v11)

Jacob was flawed. When we look back over his story, it can be hard to see past the cheating, deception, selfishness and favouritism. Yet in spite of all that, the main thing he's remembered for is blessing: the blessing he received from God, and the blessings he showered on everyone he encountered. Jacob loved to bless.

When the end is nigh for Jacob, he has the opportunity to talk to Joseph and bless his sons, Manasseh and Ephraim. You can sense the genuine feeling in the room when Jacob says, 'I never expected to see your face again, and now God has allowed me to see your children too.' The way I read this, he is choked with emotion and gratitude – he isn't stoic or pious. All those years ago, he'd lost a beloved son, only to have him returned safely (and with the added interest of two strapping grandsons). I imagine he was overwhelmed by the goodness and graciousness of God.

God is always capable of doing so much more than we think. Many times I have prayed for things with almost no hope, but have been blown away by God's generosity and kindness to me. He has practically gift-wrapped answers to prayer – things I haven't felt deserving of, but that's who He is. Other things I'm still waiting for, and that's OK.

Things don't always come instantly, obviously, or even at all in the way that we expect. But He is good. He is kind. He is faithful. He is the God of the immeasurably more (Eph. 3:20). If you're waiting, keep waiting. Jacob spent his life hoping to see his son again. And when he finally did, he got two grandsons as well.

For prayer and reflection

Spend some time reflecting on what you consider to be the greatest blessings in your life. Receive them again; give thanks again.

The last shall be **first**

Genesis 48:12–22

'Joseph said to him, "No, my father, this one is the firstborn; put your right hand on his head."'
(v18)

Despite the custom for the firstborn son to receive the double portion of blessing and inheritance, Jacob insists on blessing his grandsons in the 'wrong' order. It is a very intentional act – even though Manasseh and Ephraim are presented to him in age order, he deliberately crosses his arms to bless the youngest with the favour of his right hand. Initially, Joseph tries to correct his father, until he's reminded that there is more than enough blessing to go round: 'I know, my son... he too will become great' (v19).

As a second-born son himself, Jacob had cheated his brother Esau out of his birthright (Gen. 27), and exploited his father's poor eyesight with an elaborate deception. Perhaps in favouring the younger grandson here, he is trying to redeem the past – he wants to ensure that the youngest doesn't miss out, but he goes about it in the right way this time. It's a whisper of 'the last shall be first' (Matt. 20:16, KJV), reshuffling the traditional paradigm.

We might think we have the right to decide who 'deserves' blessing, but whether or not a person is 'worthy' is entirely to do with kingdom values, not cultural values, and Jacob understood that. Perhaps we also panic that there's a limit on just how much goodness God has to give out. Just because someone else appears to be getting a 'double portion', it doesn't mean there's not going to be enough left for you. God isn't going to run out of blessing. And if you're afraid to accept what God wants to bless you with because you think you don't deserve it, well – God has entirely different criteria. So take hold of it with both hands, and say thank you.

For prayer and reflection

God, Your way of doing things is always the best way. May my values line up with Your values. Amen.

Forgiven **for good**

'God intended it for good' (v20)

W hen we were children, if you caught us on a particularly mischievous day, my sisters and I could treat each other (and generally behave) quite differently when my parents weren't in the room. This isn't something we invented. Despite the big family reunion and lots of hugging and crying, Joseph's brothers were still wrestling with deep-seated guilt and shame, which, at Jacob's death, surfaced as fear and suspicion: 'What if Joseph holds a grudge against us and pays us back for all the wrongs we did to him?' (v15). They believed that Joseph's apparent forgiveness of them only lasted for as long as their father was alive – and now that he was out of the picture, Joseph would start dishing out the real justice. Joseph was hurt by their disbelief of his love for them: 'When their message came to him, [he] wept' (v17).

We can fall into the same trap of believing the exact same thing about God's forgiveness, as if it's something He might turn around and withdraw one day. We might question the grace that He's offered us: 'God, I know You said You'd forgiven me, but are You sure? I've done some pretty terrible things...' Just as we can reject blessing, we can end up rejecting grace.

If we really believe that God can forgive any sin and redeem any circumstance, then we have to let Him. If He really can work in any situation, then we have to trust Him with our worst experiences and toughest lessons, and believe that He can work all things for good (Rom. 8:28). There is nothing that can stop God from working things out His way – even our shortcomings, our betrayals and our failures.

**For prayer
and reflection**

**Jesus, help me to
learn how to really
receive Your
forgiveness, and to
truly let go of the
things You want to
get rid of for me.
Amen.**

A **family** portrait

When we read these verses in Hebrews, it's clear that there's a lineage of amazing faith that runs throughout the Old Testament: Abraham, Isaac, Jacob, Joseph… and later Moses, also born into a less-than-ideal situation and raised to greatness (after a period of mistakes, trials and lessons learnt). It's a hall of fame for the heroes of the faith.

After everything Joseph went through, it's not a huge surprise to see his name on the list. He went down in history as a man of great faith. In his last days, Joseph prophesied the Israelites' return home: 'God will surely come to your aid and take you up out of this land to the land he promised on oath to Abraham, Isaac and Jacob' (Gen. 50:24). He was aware that God had a big-picture plan, past and present. A legacy of faith ran through their family, as imperfect as they all were.

It's interesting to be brought back full-circle to thinking about families. Jesus' lineage boasts liars, betrayers, murderers, manipulators, prostitutes, heroes and kings. No one comes from a line of saints. My own family tree is littered with strong, faithful and clever women (with equal parts gumption and self-doubt), and godly men who served, taught and led – but they also had hang-ups and flaws to boot. None of the people listed in Hebrews 11 got there by their good behaviour. They got there because of their faith.

Perhaps you're not all that proud of where you come from, but you can be excited about where you're headed. You're part of a bigger picture, and God's plan is being worked out through you. You don't have to be brilliant – you just have to have faith.

Genesis 50:22–26; Hebrews 11:17–22

'By faith Joseph, when his end was near, spoke about the exodus of the Israelites from Egypt' (Heb. 11:22)

Amazing to confirm what I wrote in my journal before Reading this faith

For prayer and reflection

God, You know what's ahead. I put all my faith in You today. Amen.

The rescue plan

....

For reflection: Exodus 1:1–14; Isaiah 9:1–2,6–7

'Of the greatness of his government and peace there will be no end.'
(Isa. 9:7)

I t doesn't take long for things to suddenly stop looking so shiny and happy for Israel's (Jacob's) descendants. Though they begin as a collective of 70 in total (Exod. 1:5), they soon become 'far too numerous' for the Egyptians to feel comfortable. Rather than risk being outnumbered and overpowered, their strategy is to oppress the Israelites and make them slaves... for 400 years to come. But there is a plan! God will soon raise up Moses to lead the people out of slavery and towards the Promised Land.

However, Moses isn't the great man Isaiah is talking about in today's reading. Centuries after Moses, Isaiah prophesies the arrival of Jesus, who would come to emancipate all of humankind out of slavery and bondage. At the time Isaiah is talking, things don't look good. The people are crying out for a rescue plan. The good news he offers them is this: there is a plan.

God doesn't leave you in the pit or the prison. There has always been a plan to rescue you. And the kind of rescue God had in mind for you was so complete that He came down here, in the form of Jesus, to get you out Himself.

....

Optional further reflection

Listen to the song *Rescue* by Lauren Daigle (available on most streaming platforms).

Perfect Gifts for Christmas...

Advent

Journey to Christmas

For 31 days, beginning on Advent Sunday, *Journey to Christmas* by prayerfully meditating on Bible passages and reflecting on those caught up in the drama of Jesus' birth: Elizabeth and Zechariah, Mary and Joseph, the angels and the shepherds.

By Pete Greig and the 24-7 Prayer Team

ISBN: 978-1-78259-995-1

£5.99

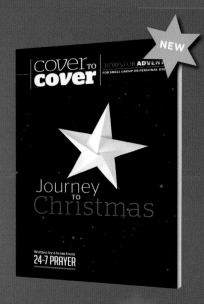

A Strange Christmas

Although the birth of Jesus fulfilled every prophecy with divine precision, none of it happened in the way the Jewish people expected. Throughout Advent, Krish Kandiah unpacks some of the 'strangeness' of the first Christmas – and how it was all part of God's plan.

By Krish Kandiah

ISBN: 978-1-78259-892-3

£5.99

For 2020

Every Day with Jesus Wall Calendar 2020: A Fresh Vision

Enjoy carefully selected Scripture verses, beautiful photographs and inspiring commentary throughout the year to come.

By Selwyn Hughes

EAN: 5027957-001725

£6.99

One Year Devotionals

One Year Devotionals

A series of pocket-sized devotional books, each comprising 365 reflections taken from issues of *Every Day with Jesus*. Each day has a specific focus and Bible reading, a key verse, reflection and a prayer.

Walking in His Ways
ISBN: 978-1-85345-314-4

A Fresh Vision of God
ISBN: 978-1-85345-121-8

Carried by Grace
ISBN: 978-1-78259-062-0

£7.99 each

Or order by post – see order form on last page

The Beauty Within
For women of all ages, this interactive, reflective journal considers how God sees us as His daughters, and how we can cultivate an inner beauty that reflects His image.
By Rosalyn Derges
ISBN: 978-1-78259-832-9
£12.99

Restoring the Balance
With so much going on, our busy lives can easily feel out of balance. Discover how to re-align yourself with God's priorities, discover real rest and re-ignite your passion for Jesus.
By Anne Le Tissier
ISBN: 978-1-78259-930-2
£7.99

The Code
Written by the team at Christian Vision for Men, this is a 12-point honour code for today's Christian man to live by, and respond to the call to live an uncompromised, Jesus-centred life.
By Carl Beech, Nathan Blackaby and Ian Manifold
ISBN: 978-1-78951-149-9
£7.99

Going Against the Grain
A refreshing take on twenty-first-century discipleship for men, and how following Jesus requires us to go against cultural norms and expectations. Ideal for men's ministry.
By Nathan Blackaby
ISBN: 978-1-78259-058-3
£7.99

Christian living

These Three Things

Exploring how we can deepen our dependence on God to meet our need for security, self-worth and significance, the seminal teaching of CWR founder Selwyn Hughes is now available as a six-week devotional journey. Designed for individuals, small groups and whole churches, this book takes an accessible approach to understanding the key elements of our personalities, and how we have been designed to find wholeness in God alone.

By Mick Brooks
ISBN: 978-1-78259-828-2
£6.99

This is Me

Whatever phase of life you're in, this journal provides space for you to write honestly. Includes thought-provoking quotes and Bible verses to help you take encouragement from the good in life, and be reminded of God's hope in the challenges.

CWR and Kintsugi Hope
ISBN: 978-1-78951-148-2
£12.99

Or order by post – see order form on last page

Christian living

These Three Things

Exploring how we can deepen our dependence on God to meet our need for security, self-worth and significance, the seminal teaching of CWR founder Selwyn Hughes is now available as a six-week devotional journey. Designed for individuals, small groups and whole churches, this book takes an accessible approach to understanding the key elements of our personalities, and how we have been designed to find wholeness in God alone.

By Mick Brooks
ISBN: 978-1-78259-828-2
£6.99

This is Me

Whatever phase of life you're in, this journal provides space for you to ~~write~~ honestly. Includes thought-~~pro~~voking quotes and Bible verses ~~help~~ you take encouragement ~~in~~ good in life, and be ~~remind~~d of God's hope in the ~~dark times~~.

~~By~~ Kintsugi Hope
~~ISBN: 978-~~1-78951-148-2

Sparky Smart from Priory Park

Follow the misadventures of Sparky (Sabrina) Smart and her family through their daily life in Priory Park. Each book contains three short stories.

By Alexa Tewkesbury

The School Fete Fiasco and Other Calamities

ISBN: 978-1-78259-929-6

The Wrong Toilet and Other Disasters

ISBN: 978-1-78259-928-9

£5.99 each

NEW

Topz Gospels: Christmas

The Topz Gang go back to Bible times to help readers grasp the true wonder of the Christmas story.

By Alexa Tewkesbury

ISBN: 978-1-78259-689-9

£5.99

50 Christmasiest Bible Stories

With colourful cartoons, Christmassy Bible stories are brought to life.

By Andy Robb

ISBN: 978-1-78259-418-5

£5.99

Topz Activity Bible

The Topz Gang retell 27 key Bible stor' the Old and New Testament, bringing Word to life.

By Alexa Tewkesbury

ISBN: 978-1-78259-419-2

£8.99

For young people and families

One You, One Year

These one-year devotionals are packed with inspiring Bible readings, relevant thinking points and life-changing prayers. Written in an engaging and upbeat style with specific themes, these books will encourage young people in their walk with God.

Ideal for ages 10–14

One You, One Year: 365 for Boys
ISBN: 978-1-78259-994-4

One You, One Year: 365 for Girls
ISBN: 978-1-78259-993-7

£9.99 each

Family Devotionals

These family devotionals each include 12 weeks of daily Bible readings, thoughts and activities for the whole family to enjoy together. Written with insights from the authors' own family. The three titles can be read in any order.
By Steve and Bekah Legg

All Together
ISBN: 978-1-78259-692-9

Time Together
ISBN: 978-1-78259-798-8

Life Together
ISBN: 978-1-78259-999-9

£8.99 each

Or order by post – see order form on last page

The Beauty Within

For women of all ages, this interactive, reflective journal considers how God sees us as His daughters, and how we can cultivate an inner beauty that reflects His image.

By Rosalyn Derges

ISBN: 978-1-78259-832-9

£12.99

Restoring the Balance

With so much going on, our busy lives can easily feel out of balance. Discover how to re-align yourself with God's priorities, discover real rest and re-ignite your passion for Jesus.

By Anne Le Tissier

ISBN: 978-1-78259-930-2

£7.99

The Code

Written by the team at Christian Vision for Men, this is a 12-point honour code for today's Christian man to live by, and respond to the call to live an uncompromised, Jesus-centred life.

By Carl Beech, Nathan Blackaby and Ian Manifold

ISBN: 978-1-78951-149-9

£7.99

Going Against the Grain

A refreshing take on twenty-first-century discipleship for men, and how following Jesus requires us to go against cultural norms and expectations. Ideal for men's ministry.

By Nathan Blackaby

ISBN: 978-1-78259-058-3

£7.99

No Greater Love

LYN GITCHEL

**Song of Songs
2:1–7**

'Let him lead me to
the banquet hall,
and let his banner
over me be love.'
(v4)

A meal is often the start of a lasting friendship. Sometimes the invitation to have a meal with someone is the beginning of something far deeper, and during that mealtime a love relationship might be birthed. When Jesus said, 'I stand at the door and knock. If anyone hears my voice and opens the door, I will come in', He did not stop there. He went on to say, 'I will come in and eat with that person, and they with me' (Rev. 3:20). Sometimes people stop at 'I will come in' and miss the significance of the rest of what Jesus is actually saying.

You might not make it a habit to sit and eat with your boss, or someone else who has a position of authority over you, but when you're with a friend it is different. You enjoy time spent together, and often you spend that time having a meal together. When Jesus speaks to the unbeliever, or even to a believer, and asks him or her to open the door, He is initiating a relationship – a love relationship. He is asking to be your friend; He is asking permission to move into your life and heart in a relationship that will grow deeper and deeper as you spend time with Him. That's how a love relationship develops: by spending time, quality time, together. This month, let's do just that: spend time with Him and let that love develop and deepen. Let's plan to take a little extra time each day to chat with the Lord about what goes on in our lives. Let's not just rush into His presence with a list of prayer requests and out again. He deserves more. Let's really take the time to develop a love relationship with Him.

**For prayer
and reflection**

Yes, Lord, that's
what I really want:
to develop a love
relationship with
You. Help me to
remember to
spend time with
You in order to let
it happen. Amen.

Love's **fellowship**

Zephaniah 3:14–17

'He will take great delight in you; in his love he will… rejoice over you with singing.' (v17)

I often smile at the length of time young couples in love take to say goodbye to each other. Many don't seem to actually say much at all, but still prolong the parting as long as possible, whispering sweet nothings in each other's ears or simply holding each other in a comfortable silence. It's not only young people who delight in each other's company in this way either. People who are in love can spend hours just being together, saying little or nothing, but with a deep bond of love flowing between them. 'Togetherness' is a word often used and it describes just that: the joy of simply being together.

Does it surprise you to know that the Lord enjoys our company in this way? It is not hard to see how we can enjoy His presence and feel blessed just to be near Him. Sometimes His presence is so real that we simply bask in it saying nothing, just enjoying His nearness. But the wonder of it is that God enjoys this kind of fellowship with us, too. Isn't that incredible? Can you imagine the great Almighty God enjoying the company of one small creature so much that He says He 'will take great delight in you' and will even 'rejoice over you with singing'?

The King James Version has an even more amazing translation of part of this verse that says, 'he will rest in his love'. Doesn't that bring up the picture of two people, sitting together, perhaps on a sunny hillside, and simply enjoying each other's company, not bothering even to say much to each other, just being together? And, remember, these words are spoken by the great God of the universe to a tiny human being – to you or me!

For prayer and reflection

Wow, Lord, that's incredible – that you would actually enjoy my company! May I never lose the wonder of that. Amen.

Exciting plans for 2020 and beyond

As part of our 'Vision 2020', we will be bringing some of our key teaching to several cities around the UK. Our partnerships with various churches and organisations, including Kintsugi Hope, have enabled us to bring to fruition our hopes to meet and resource as many of you as we can.

We will be holding conferences in Bristol, Birmingham and Bradford, with plans for Belfast and Edinburgh too.

Seminars and events will include:

- **Inspiring Women** seminars, days and weekends
- **Insight Days** – initially covering Anxiety, Depression, Shame and Perfectionism
- **Honesty Over Silence** conferences – addressing issues around our mental health and wellbeing
- **These Three Things** – bringing our updated teaching on where we find our security, self-worth and significance
- **Introduction to Christian Care and Counselling** – our one-week counselling course

We look forward to meeting you!

To find out more, book your place, or request to host an event, visit **cwr.org.uk/courses** or call **+44 (0)1252 784719**

Love's **security**

1 John 4:16–18

'There is no fear in love. But perfect love drives out fear' (v18)

This familiar verse is often quoted as an antidote to the many fears put upon us by our enemy to hold us back from doing what God wants us to do, or to be what He wants us to be. This scripture assures us that as our love for the Lord increases, many of our own fears will simply fade away, and so they will. 'The expulsive power of a new affection' was the way the great Scottish minister Thomas Chalmers described this phenomenon. But let's look at this verse from another angle.

Does it surprise you that this is also true of God? Perfect love is the kind of love that knows no fear, and the love that God has for us is perfect. God has no fear in His heart, only trust – and that trust is centered on you and on me. He believes in us! He has confidence in us! Would you not think that God would be afraid that we would let Him down, or, knowing the frailty of human nature, be afraid that our love would grow cold? Would you not think that He would fear that we would put some other person or activity before Him and push Him out of the centre of our lives? But no – God's love is perfect love and knows no fear.

I have a son who found himself in a mess of his own making for many years. He ended up in prison for quite a long period of his life, but it did not make me love him any less, and I always had confidence that one day he would find God and turn things around, becoming a whole person, loving and serving the Lord. And he did. It took many years, but he did.

God's love is perfect. He has no fear that we will fail him. He believes in each one of us and loves us through every difficulty.

For prayer and reflection

Lord, You are so amazing. You really trust me, believe in me, have confidence in me. Help me to live up to what You expect of me. Amen.

Love's **comfort**

**Philippians
2:1–11**

'if you have any
encouragement
from being united
with Christ, if any
comfort from his
love…' (v1)

O f all the wonderful things about being loved, one of the most wonderful is the sense of security and comfort that it brings. No matter what comes or what happens, we rest in the sure and certain knowledge that we are deeply cared for by those that love us. This fact brings a deep comfort, yet how much truer it is when we rest in the knowledge that we are loved by God with a love that is far richer than any human love!

I recently read an article about young criminal offenders, and it was printed under the headline, 'Hungry for love'. Some might have wondered what that heading had to do with a feature on juvenile delinquency, but I think it had profound significance. For sure, one of the greatest things lacking in so many young lives is the sense of being loved and the security that it can bring with it. Somehow, when we know we're loved, it has an influence over every area of our lives, including our behaviour.

The epistle to the Philippians was written to Christians during a time of fierce persecution. It was not easy to be a Christian then – dangerous, even. But what would have made it all worth it was the comforting assurance of being loved eternally and unconditionally by the God of love. This knowledge would have brought a deep feeling of security in the midst of not knowing what the next day would bring, or if there would even be a 'next day'. Despite not knowing how long their lives would be spared, the Philippian Christians knew they were loved. No matter what happened, they could rest on the fact that God loved each one of them with a love so deep and boundless that it could carry them through.

**For prayer
and reflection**

Lord, Your love
amazes me – that
You could love us,
mere specks on
this earth in the
boundless
universe. But I
know You do, so
help me to fully
realise it in my
own life. Amen.

Love's **proof**

Romans 5:6–11

'But God demonstrates his own love for us in this: While we were still sinners, Christ died for us.' (v8)

t's not difficult to love someone who is sweet and kind, but to love a person who appears to embody only evil and unpleasantness seems humanly impossible. The best proof of the wonder and greatness of the love of God is that it was not after we came to know Him and were born again that He loved us, but before – while we were still living a sinful life without Him.

Take Paul, for example. He was breathing out murderous threats against the very people God had given His Son to redeem. Paul, then known as Saul, was torturing and killing these followers of Jesus as fast as he could find them. Some may even liken the fervour and zealousness behind Paul's intention to destroy the early Christians to Hitler's efforts to destroy the Jews, or the abhorrent attacks by ISIS in the Middle East. To us, it is impossible to imagine that an individual as repulsive to us as Hitler was could have ever turned to the Lord, but Paul did – and it was while he was on his way to Damascus to kill Christians that Jesus met Him.

It is hard to think of Paul in this ugly light because we have seen how God transformed his life, but the comparison makes a good illustration. Can you imagine loving someone so evil, so much that you would give your life for him like Jesus did? God *did*. He gave His Son to die in the place of even the most sinful so that they might spend eternity with Him. That's God's kind of extreme love, love for the worst of sinners, love that reaches out and wins them to Himself. It happened in the life of Paul, the great persecutor of Christians, and it happened for every person who has ever walked this earth.

For prayer and reflection

Thank You, Lord, for not turning Your back on me. Thank You for loving me. I am so grateful to You for Your love. Amen.

Love's forgiveness

....

For reflection: Luke 23:26–36

'Father, forgive them, for they do not know what they are doing.' (v34)

We might think that God's forgiveness is entirely dependent upon us – that we need to straighten out our lives and become 'perfect' before we are deserving of His forgiveness. But because of what Jesus did on the cross, we are already forgiven. All we need do is receive it: 'If we confess our sins, he is faithful and just and will forgive us' (1 John 1:9). The forgiveness of God is the result of His love alone.

By our own standards, and our human understanding of justice, to reject and crucify Jesus is surely unforgivable. To take the one who had come to earth to bring nothing but love, the one who had healed the sick and fed the hungry multitudes, and kill Him in the most brutal and humiliating fashion – that surely could be said to be unforgivable. Yet Jesus cried out, 'Father, forgive them', even then. In fact, the Greek word *aorist* used in Luke's Gospel account is the past-continual tense. Jesus shouted it not just once, but went on crying out, 'Father, forgive them.' Surely there is no greater love.

....

Optional further reflection

Spend some time in God's presence, thanking Him for His forgiveness towards you. Ask Him to prompt you if there's anyone in your own life you need to forgive.

Love's **faithfulness**

Lamentations 3:19–33

'Because of the LORD's great love we are not consumed, for his compassions never fail. They are new every morning' (vv22–23)

Human relationships try us, and we can often find ourselves losing patience with someone. There are some people we find more annoying than others – in fact, as someone has said, there are some people whose ministry seems to be that of working patience in others!

Love is one of the wonderful things that almost completely solves the difficulty. Perhaps you have met a married couple, one of whom tried your patience in a most annoying manner and left you wondering what their partner sees in her or him. The answer lies in the love that flows between them. When you love someone enough, no matter how annoying they may seem to others, there is very little of it that touches you. As the saying goes, it's like water off a duck's back. The annoyance rides on top of the flow of love, scarcely affecting or touching the perfection of that love underneath it.

We say that God is patient with us, and so He is – but the picture here is not of a father who is frustrated over an erring child, demanding all the patience he can muster, but a picture of a loving heavenly Father who scarcely notices how many times we fail. It is the perfect patience of His deep, deep love. In fact, even if it were possible to out-sin the patience of God, His compassions are new every morning, so by the following morning it would all be over and forgotten and a new day begun. It's not possible: you cannot exhaust the loving forgiveness of God. He never says, 'What, not again!' His love is so perfect that He just keeps on loving and forgiving, no matter how often it has to happen.

For prayer and reflection

Heavenly Father, Your patience is so wonderful. I am so grateful to You that You do not give up when I get things wrong. Thank You for Your love. Amen.

Waverley Abbey College

Would you like to be equipped to…
- develop your pastoral care skills?
- become a professional counsellor?
- mentor and coach others?
- help others find purpose through spiritual direction?

As the educational arm of CWR, Waverley Abbey College provides university validated part-time undergraduate and postgraduate Higher Education programmes in both Counselling and Spiritual Formation. There are also vocational courses that can be taken to provide more rounded experience and knowledge, or as pathways to Higher Education.

Introduction to Christian Care and Counselling (ICCC)

The five-day ICCC course teaches foundational counselling principles within a sound Christian context. Learn more about yourself, how to listen to others more effectively and how to support people in everyday life.

Waverley Abbey College Open Days

Come to a free Open Day to find out more, meet tutors, explore Waverley Abbey House and hear what makes our training unique.

To find out more or to register for an Open Day, call **01252 784731** or visit **waverleyabbeycollege.ac.uk** or email **registry@waverleyabbeycollege.ac.uk**

Love's **boundlessness**

Jeremiah 31:1–9

'I have loved you with an everlasting love; I have drawn you with unfailing kindness.' (v3)

t is almost beyond our understanding to comprehend the love of God. We either take it hopelessly for granted or brush it aside as something we cannot understand. There are so many facets of that great love and so little of it is comparable to anything in our own experience.

One of the things found in the love of God alone is the fact that no matter how often we hurt Him, He goes on loving us just the same. Humans cannot claim a love like that. We may put up with a lot of hurt from someone, but to keep on loving them unconditionally, to the exact same extent and in our own strength, is not within our human capability. Some people do have a deep love coupled with a great deal of patience; they are optimistic at heart and do not easily give up. Others go on loving because they have no one else to turn to. But even then, in all of us, there is a deep reaction to being hurt that makes it difficult to trust the other person and which numbs the heart and cools the love we have for that person.

But God is not like that. His love for us draws Him ceaselessly to us – just as His love also draws us to Him, though that may be a long process with some of us. It is as if He is saying, 'I would rather have you be mine with all the hurt it causes me than to live without you.' That was the message of the cross, with all its suffering, that Jesus went through. It was His intense love for us sinful human beings, and the potential of winning us to Himself, that drove Him to sacrifice everything.

How great is the love of God, and how abundant the flow of all that God longs to pour into our lives. His love is everlasting.

For prayer and reflection

Lord God, You are so amazing! You have always loved me, though I have not always appreciated it. Help me to return Your love more fully. Amen.

Love's **gentleness**

G od used the life of the prophet Hosea to demonstrate how patient and gentle His love is with us, even when we keep going astray.

When God needs to bring to our attention a sin or wrongdoing that needs addressing, He does so with gentleness. I remember when I first realised this: it was a time when the Lord woke me in the middle of the night to make me aware of something that I needed to put right with Him there and then. The next day, Sunday, I listened to a sermon that dealt with the very same thing, culminating in an altar call for those who wanted to put that error right in their lives. How thankful I was that in my heart I had the sure and certain knowledge that I had already set this right with God. Why did He not wait and tell me the following day in the sermon? For me, our quiet exchange in the night was the gentlest way that He could deal with me.

After King David stole Uriah's wife and subsequently arranged his murder, God chose a different way to get through to him. He sent the prophet Nathan to David with a parable – the story of a greedy man who had all he needed but still wanted one poor man's only lamb. Using a picture of his own covetousness, the Holy Spirit brought conviction to David's heart and he repented in earnest. At the end of his life, King David was able to say, 'your gentleness has made me great!' (2 Sam. 22:36, NKJV). David knew that in all His dealings with him, God had used the gentlest method He could. We need not fear God's dealings with us. He is so gentle.

Hosea 11:1–4

'To them I was like one who lifts a little child to the cheek' (v4)

For prayer and reflection

Thank You, Lord, for Your gentleness. Help me to understand and grasp more of Your incredible love. Amen.

Love's **persistence**

2 Corinthians
5:11–15

'For Christ's love
compels us' (v14)

I n the original language, the word in this passage now translated as 'compels' is a strong one, along the lines of 'irresistible'. This word has been used very few times in Scripture, but one example is when it was used to describe Peter's mother-in-law before Jesus healed her (Luke 4:38). The King James Version translates that same word by saying that she was 'taken with a great fever', which suggests that she was hopelessly in the grip of her illness.

In the dictionary, the meaning of the word 'compels' is to drive or urge forcefully or irresistibly. The word 'constrain' has a similar meaning, and the King James Version actually renders today's focus verse as: 'the love of Christ constraineth us'. The love of Jesus is just like that. We are in its grip; we cannot escape it; we are unable to resist. Some may try to break 'free', turning their backs on the Lord, but that love holds onto them just the same.

Jeremiah also found this to be true. Look at Jeremiah 20:9: 'But if I say, "I will not mention his word or speak any more in his name," his word is in my heart like a fire, a fire shut up in my bones. I am weary of holding it in; indeed, I cannot.' Notice how Jeremiah says it wearies him more to fight God than to be persecuted for delivering His message, as he would have been at that time. How true this is! The love of Christ within us is so forceful that to fight Him makes us unhappier than any trials or troubles we might meet with through serving Him. Whatever you are currently facing, may that encourage you.

**For prayer
and reflection**

Lord, it's so true.
There have been
times when I have
turned my back on
You, but You have
not let me go.
I worship You.
Amen.

Love's **strength**

**Song of Songs
8:5-7**

'Place me like a seal
over your heart,
like a seal on your
arm; for love is as
strong as death'
(v6)

I used to think that this verse meant that love was strong enough to go through death and die for the one it loves, to lay down its life for the good of the other person. That would indeed be wonderful, and of course it was God's love that caused Jesus to be willing to endure the awful pain and death of the cross for us – but this verse does not say that. The verse is likening the strength of love to the *strength* of death. Simply that: as strong as death is, that's how strong God's love is.

Think about it. Can you think of anything that has more grip on us humans than death? Anything else that simply cannot be broken? Death can be delayed sometimes, but it is still inevitable. Is there anything else that you or even others fighting for you simply cannot resist once it holds you in its grasp? The Bible says God's love is that strong! His love has a grip that cannot be released by any human means. If you have ever felt the grip of real love in your life, you begin to know how true this is – even with limited, human love. And God's love is far stronger even than that, because His love is perfect.

Once you are in the grip of God's love, you cannot loosen the hold it has on your life. You may not always be aware of it, and perhaps that's why the Bible is so insistent in its reminder to us that it is there, and it is this strong. You are in its grip and nothing you can ever do will change that. You cannot resist it; in the end you will have to yield to it. This is the strength of the love God has for you!

**For prayer
and reflection**

Father God, I yield to Your amazing love. It's hard to believe You love me that much, but if the Bible says it, I believe it. Help me live in the realisation of it. Amen.

Weekend

Love's responsibility

....

For reflection: 1 John 3:1–3

'See what great love the Father has lavished on us, that we should be called children of God!' (v1)

It is wonderful that God loved us enough to work out our salvation, but the wonder does not stop there. Still more wonderful is the fact that God chose to make us part of His plan. He might have been better off, we might think, if He had planned to work His own purposes out here on this earth, without having our weaknesses to contend with. But no! God has chosen that His redeemed people should be vital to His purposes for this world. In other words, God has a business to run here on this earth, and He has left us in charge of running it. He has not left us entirely unsupervised, but there is work to be done, with His help and in His strength.

God wants us to seize our responsibility with joy and play our part in bringing others into a relationship with Jesus, not simply to rest in the comfortable and enjoyable knowledge that we will spend eternity in heaven. Heaven is a reality, but there is work to be done in God's business here and now. This weekend, spend some time asking God what He has for you to do, and embrace the responsibility.

....

Optional further reading
Romans 8:14–21

Restore and Release.

A gift to the next generation

So much of CWR's ministry is only possible because of the generosity, prayers and support of those who leave us gifts in their will. Imagine the difference that could be made by your legacy...

Be the reason a child gets to know Jesus

Help someone overcome anxiety, depression or grief with our Christian counselling training

Send life-changing biblical resources into prisons

Include a gift to CWR in your will and you can help enable us to continue:

Helping people to apply God's Word to their daily lives

Serving the Church with resources and teaching

Equipping counsellors to help people live their lives to the fullness God intended

The legacies that CWR supporters leave us enable us to respond to God's call to continue serving His people. After you've taken care of loved ones, would you consider leaving a gift to CWR in your will to help preserve and grow our work for future generations?

••

Please get in touch if you have any questions, or would like to know more about leaving a gift to CWR in your will.

Email **partners@cwr.org.uk** or call **+44 (0)1252 784709.**

Love's **privilege**

Ephesians 1:3–14

'In love he predestined us for adoption to sonship through Jesus Christ, in accordance with his pleasure and will' (vv4–5)

What an amazing thought this is: not only did Jesus redeem us and put us back into the right relationship with God the Father, but He lifted us right out of our present surroundings and put us into a new relationship with Himself, the Son, as well.

Say, for example, that you wanted to help support an orphaned child. If you wanted to do so from a distance, you could give money regularly, covering living costs and other expenses. You could gladly pay for the child's keep and education, and might be depended on financially for food, clothing and any other material needs while he or she is in the care of a home or organisation. While this is significant and very generous, it is not always possible for there to be much of a relationship between you and the child in question. But there is also another way. When they feel called to do so, some people adopt the child and bring him or her into their own family. They set the child beside their own children as one of the family in every way. The child takes the parents' name and truly becomes one of them. An adopted child then has the same legal rights as any other children, and must be treated equally as one of them.

This is exactly what God has done for us. He did not just make it possible for us make heaven our home. The death and resurrection of Jesus has indeed made that possible, but that's not all. We have been taken out of our old lives as ordinary human people, lifted into a totally new family life and set beside the Son of God in God's heavenly family. Because of Jesus, we are now equally accepted in God's sight, just as Jesus is.

For prayer and reflection

Lord, I never cease to be amazed at what You have done for me! The hope of heaven is wonderful, but this is even more wonderful – to be part of Your family. Amen.

Love's **rebuke**

W e all go through difficulties in life but often, when we try to look at a tough situation from God's point of view, it can become a lot more acceptable to us. Consider, for example, when you feel that Satan is attacking your work, your family or your life. How depressing it seems, and how impossible to succeed or to achieve anything worthwhile. But, as I have heard it suggested, perhaps our enemy is particularly on the prowl against those who are actively embracing their role in God's kingdom plan. Have there been times in your life when you have been working hard for the Lord, but felt as if you have a spiritual 'target' on your back? We have a real and active enemy, and when we remember this at times when we feel under attack, we might even be encouraged by the possibility that he is annoyed by what God is doing in us and through us.

With correction that comes from God through the Holy Spirit there is also deep encouragement to be found when we look at it with a divine perspective. It isn't ever nice to be corrected or told that what we are doing isn't quite right, and we don't tend to enjoy the feeling of being convicted – no matter how gently that conviction comes. Our natural reaction might inititally be to sulk or try to justify our behaviour, yet God's love is patient and wins our hearts to His will. As we see God's side of the story, we understand that He only bothers to correct us because He has confidence in us and believes that we will fall in line with His plan for our lives.

> **Revelation
> 3:18–22**
>
> 'Those whom I love
> I rebuke and
> discipline.' (v19)

For prayer and reflection

Help me, Father, to try to look at things from Your point of view. Help me to know that even the unpleasant things in life can be a cause for joy when looked at this way. Amen.

Love's **defence**

1 John 2:1–6

'But if anyone obeys his word, love for God is truly made complete in them.' (v5)

One of the things that made Jesus the perfect image of God was the fact that there was never a single moment in His life that was out of sync with God. 'I do nothing on my own but speak just what the Father has taught me', was the claim Jesus made (John 8:28), and, 'Very truly I tell you, the Son can do nothing by himself; he can do only what he sees his Father doing, because whatever the Father does the Son also does' (John 5:19). And again: 'By myself I can do nothing; I judge only as I hear, and my judgment is just, for I seek not to please myself but him who sent me' (John 5:30). These statements give us a perfect picture of the perfect obedience of the perfect Son. And the reason that Jesus was able to stay in the will of God so perfectly was this: the love that flowed between the Father and the Son was perfect too.

When you love someone deeply, you cultivate a way of thinking where, before doing or saying anything, you consider how the other person will feel about it and how it will affect them. If it will hurt them, you do not do it. If it will please them, then that makes all the difference. This is true of Jesus. He would do nothing that would hurt His Father and He lived His whole life to please Him. He found out what the Father wanted Him to do and then did only that, regardless of how He Himself was feeling about it. If only we could cultivate for ourselves the habit of thinking first – of thinking in love about everything we do – then our lives would flow out with love to those around us and, in turn, would give back more love to God.

For prayer and reflection

Help me, Father, to think first in everything that I do, so that I may always do what You want. Amen.

Love's **compassion**

'When Jesus landed and saw a large crowd, he had compassion on them, because they were like sheep without a shepherd.' (v34)

At this point in Mark's Gospel, Jesus had had no time to Himself for some time. Scripture tells us that 'so many people were coming and going that they did not even have a chance to eat'. Furthermore, Jesus was sad and upset because King Herod had just killed His cousin and friend, John the Baptist, and so He had withdrawn to try to find some time alone (Matt. 14:12–14). The disciples had been away from Jesus for some time and now they had just returned. Probably wanting to spend time alone with them and to hear their report, Jesus said, 'Come with me by yourselves to a quiet place and get some rest.' But a crowd of more than five thousand people followed, awaiting them on the shore before they'd even landed the boat.

So much for time in a quiet place! Most of us would have been thoroughly disappointed at having to abandon our brief opportunity to relax. Our hearts would have sunk and we probably would have cried out, 'Oh no!' Maybe Jesus did too – after all, He was human – but we do know that His loving nature immediately took over, and He felt for the people instead of Himself. 'He had compassion on them', we read, because He saw their deep need. He was tired and He was sad, but love took over and He taught them and ministered to them.

Not only did Jesus give of Himself that day, but He also gave out food in abundance! If you read on, you find that He taught them until the end of the day and then asked His followers to go and get the food they had brought with them. When they brought their small supper to Him, He divided that among the crowd and fed them all. Even His miracles are compassionate!

For prayer and reflection

Lord, I see how love can take over. Give me a selfless compassion for others, that I may focus on their needs instead of my own. Amen.

Love's **depth**

Hosea 2:16–3:1

'The LORD said to me, "Go, show your love to your wife again, though she is loved by another"' (3:1)

Οne of the most wonderful things about God is this: when we come to Him for forgiveness, He grants it. Though we may have sinned many times and might expect Him to say, 'Not again!', each time, with God, it is as if it is the first time. He said of the Israelites that He would 'remember their sins no more' (Jer. 31:34). Note that God does not say He had forgotten them, for a forgotten thing can always be recalled again later. God goes one step further than that and says He determines not to remember it, even when He is reminded of it. To 'remember no more' is an active thing, a determination not to bring it to mind. God has pushed the sin right out of His thinking and it is as if it has never happened. Sometimes the Bible refers to it as 'justified'; just-as-if-I'd never sinned.

In this chapter of Hosea, we have an illustration of the love of God. Hosea's wife had left him and was living with another man. When the Bible tells how God asked Hosea to go and get her back, it is clear about the details. It wasn't after she had broken off the relationship – it was while she was still in the throes of the affair – yet Hosea was told to go and get her and love her. It was that point that illustrated the love of God. He doesn't wait for us to repent and turn back to Him; He goes on loving and forgiving. The decision to respond is ours, because God has loved us all along. Hosea was told to go and get his wife back and, not only that, but to love her and treat her as though the affair had never happened. What a task for a husband! But how perfect an illustration of the depth of the love of God.

For prayer and reflection

Lord, it is almost impossible to understand how great and how perfect Your love is! Help me to grasp a little more of it today. Amen.

Love's source

....

For reflection: 1 John 4:7–18

'God is love.' (v8)

Many things in our human experience can draw from our own hearts an answering love. A baby's smile, a loved one's hand, a dog's eyes, a smile, a tear – all these reach into our hearts and call forth our love. But nothing in the realm of humanity calls forth love from God because He is the *source* of all love. He created us in love; He pursues us in love. God pours out His love upon us to win us back into the abundance of His full and perfect life.

Nothing demonstrates this more fully and obviously than Jesus laying down His life for us. It is beyond our understanding that God could love a broken world so much that He would give His own Son, sending Him into the world as a baby to grow up among us and then die for us – yet that is the God we serve. As we embrace the excitement of Christmas this week, let's remember that God is the source of all love, and has given Jesus for us as the ultimate gift. Whatever other love we may give, receive, share and enjoy, He is the source of it all. And when we don't feel that we have enough love to give, let's tap into the source.

....

Optional further reflection

Write a love letter to God, then fold it and keep it in your Bible.

Love's **fulfilment**

Galatians 4:3–5

'But when the set time had fully come, God sent his Son' (v4)

There really was no greater gift that God could have given. Can you imagine, from a human point of view, giving away your son to someone else? Furthermore, how about doing so knowing that many would reject him and despise him? Surely that goes against our every instinct – who could we love more than our own son? Further still, how about doing so knowing that he would suffer cruelly at the hands of the people to whom you have given him? It's a harrowing thought, and one we shudder at.

Yet this was the ultimate fulfilment, the absolute manifestation of the extent of God's love towards His fallen creation – towards you and me. And the timing of this, we read in verse 4, was fixed and specific. God chose that exact moment in human history to send to us the gift of our Messiah. We were 'in slavery under the elemental spiritual forces' (v3), but God has bought our freedom. We are free!

As Christmas Day approaches, with all its sparkle and distraction, let's determine to keep that gift foremost in our own lives. Let's allow the reality of it to permeate our hearts and create in each of us a sense of profound thankfulness and worship, since worship is our own way of expressing appreciation to God and thanks for what He has done. Why not try to find a way to give back to Him today? Be creative in expressing your love to Him. If love's fulfilment came through Jesus' sacrifice let's practise sacrificial love this Christmas. And as you prepare to give gifts to those you love in the next couple of days, why not consider an offering to Jesus too? What is He asking of You today?

For prayer and reflection

Dear Father God, help me to give back to You in some special way. May Your incredible gift to me be the main thing I celebrate this Christmas. Amen.

Next Issue

January

THE WOMEN OF LUKE'S GOSPEL

CAROLINE FLETCHER

February

SONGS OF LIFE

ROSALYN DERGES

In January, Caroline Fletcher celebrates the women of Luke's Gospel who encountered Jesus – those who anticipated His birth, sat at His feet, worshipped Him and followed Him.

In February, Rosalyn Derges explores the beauty and depth of the Psalms, and discovers honest songs of hope, joy, lament and thanksgiving, all of which speak of a faithful God.

Also available as eBook/eSubscription

Obtain your copy from CWR, Christian bookshops or your National Distributor.
If you would like to take out a subscription, see the order form at the back of these notes.

Love's **choice**

Philippians 2:5–11

'he made himself nothing by taking the very nature of a servant, being made in human likeness' (v7)

I heard a Christmas song the other day, but it was rather unusual. It was sung from the perspective of Joseph, husband of Mary, expressing the way he felt about the coming of Jesus, and God giving His own Son. The lyrics, 'What a strange way to save the world', were repeated several times throughout, along with Joseph's words expressing amazement that God would have chosen to send His Son into the world as a tiny, vulnerable baby, dependent upon ordinary people to raise Him with all the indignities of human life. He truly was 'made in human likeness'.

Let's be honest – if you or I had arranged to send God's Son into the world, we probably would have chosen a magnificent palace and had Him arrive in splendor with all the regality of a king... not a humble manger as a bed after being refused a place at the local lodging house. It's almost as if God couldn't have stretched any further than that – it was as humble and as extreme as He could go. It is as if God said, 'See how much I love you!' and brought forth a tiny, helpless, utterly dependent newborn baby. He was born a king, not in a royal palace like we might expect, but in the most humble surroundings God could have thought up. It was no mistake that there was no room in the lodging house; it was typical of the path Jesus would walk. It was also no mistake that a life of rejection by religious leaders, who should have known better, ended on a cross. It was the way God wrapped up this gift He gave, wrapped up to bear the sins of mankind. A tiny baby with the weight of the world resting on His shoulders.

For prayer and reflection

Father, I see now why You did it – why You chose to come to us in this perfectly imperfect way. All I can do is wonder! Amen.

Love **manifested**

Luke 2:1–16

'She wrapped him in cloths and placed him in a manger, because there was no guest room available for them.' (v7)

Though the Bible doesn't explicitly say, tradition has always said that Mary and Joseph sheltered in a stable for the birth of Jesus (which would explain the manger in which He slept). Some suggest that this also might have been a cave, or even a private outbuilding. But what we do know is this: Jesus, the Son of God, was laid in a manger because that's all that was available. In lowly surroundings, in the company of the displaced, the shepherds would have felt very at home. As the very first people to whom any announcement of a Saviour was made, they needed to be able to approach the cradle of Jesus – somewhat complicated if He had been born in a palace!

While we considered yesterday what Joseph might have thought about the extremes to which God went to express His love, today we think about the shepherds. The angels had told them that this baby was the long-awaited Saviour, and also said they'd find Him bedded down in a manger. Strange, but wonderful! How blown away must they have been? Not only had the long-awaited Messiah finally arrived, but they, on the bottom rung of the social ladder, were to be the very first visitors to the delivery room. This is a holy, awesome and divine love that transcends any social barriers: a royalty that trumps any hierarchy or riches. God was not concerned with showing off His Son to the big-wigs of the day – He was (and still is) first and foremost interested in the lowly, the humble and the obedient. God is not bound by our expectations – in fact, He can often be found where we least expect to find Him.

For prayer and reflection

Lord Jesus, thank You for Your incredible gift of perfect love. I worship You today. Amen.

Love's **plan**

'For God so loved the world that he gave his one and only Son' (v16)

God had it all planned, and it was a unique plan that only God could have thought up. This baby, this gift to mankind, was to be a substitute for all the wrong and sin of the world. He would grow up to be a man – a perfect man shaped and moulded by God, who would teach, heal and show people how to live and how it should be done. But they would not listen. Ultimately, they would kill Him to silence Him.

But it didn't silence God's plan. It was part of it. The gift of a baby in a manger was one part of it. The life, the healing and the teaching were another. Jesus' death was also a part of the plan, an exchange plan. The Bible says that God laid on Jesus the sin of all humanity and, in exchange, took from Jesus His perfect life and laid it on us, a gift of righteousness (see Isa. 53:6). But that wasn't the only gift, this gift of righteousness. Romans 5:17–18 refers to another gift, the gift of justification: 'For if by one man's offence death reigned by one; much more they which receive abundance of grace and of the gift of righteousness shall reign in life by one, Jesus Christ... by the righteousness of one the free gift came upon all men unto justification of life' (KJV). Justification means that the perfect life of Jesus was accounted to each believer, and now, when God looks on each of us, He sees the covering of the righteousness of Jesus.

God didn't have to do any of this, so why did He? Love. For God *so loved the world*. Truly, there is no greater love than this.

For prayer and reflection

Wow, God, You are awesome! Thank You so much that Your plan reaches even to me, today. Amen.

Love worth **knowing**

God never intended for this love, the love that He showed by giving His Son to and for the world, to be a one-sided thing. Love is meant to be shared, to be returned. We all know that God has commanded over and over again that love be the essence of our Christian walk – love towards Him and also towards each other. But sometimes it seems we don't know what this really means, that we don't know what is required of us and how a person can love a being that we have never even seen.

Some aspects of the media seem to champion the idea that love and sex are the same thing, clouding the truth of what love is really all about. In 'the Hollywood version' of love, relationships are about what we can get from the other person, and not what we can give. Our culture teaches us that love is an emotion – something you fall into – but that's not entirely true either. Emotions are transitory and may only stick around for a short while... and then what? When we understand that love is a choice – an active decision we can make each day – it is suddenly much more meaningful.

In his letter to the Ephesians, Paul exhorts his fellow Christians to be 'rooted and established in love'. This is not the kind of fickle, fleeting, romantic love that we might like to idealise in fiction. This is the love of God – too wide, long, high and deep for us to get our heads around – the love in which we are to root ourselves. Loving other people can be hard – particularly when they hurt or frustrate us. But when we are 'rooted and established' in the love of God, who can do 'immeasurably more' (Eph. 3:20) than we can imagine, anything is possible.

Ephesians 3:16–20

'I pray that you, being rooted and established in love, may... grasp how wide and long and high and deep is the love of Christ.' (vv17–18)

For prayer and reflection

Heavenly Father, help me to learn to love deeply and truly in the way You do. Amen.

Love in relationship

....

For reflection: 1 John 4:11–21

'God is love. Whoever lives in love lives in God, and God in them.'
(v16)

I want to return again to 1 John 4, as it's such a great chapter. When we think about today's focus verse, it must above all things refer to the God kind of love and not the Hollywood kind. The writer is not saying that when we have a romantic relationship with someone, God is automatically part of it. That is backwards. God has to come at the beginning as we consider what a love relationship is. It begins with God.

Let's think about a love relationship as best we know it. First, you spend time with the person you love – and not just time spent asking for things (though this is how a lot of people seem to treat God). A true love relationship simply enjoys the other person's presence, enjoying hearing what is going on in the other person's life, and is built upon mutual trust, openness and honesty. We talk about small and seemingly trivial things, as well as more important issues. Why not try this with God this weekend? Tell Him about your day and share with Him the things that have brought pleasure to you. And listen. Just listen. If you listen He will talk with you. Try it and see.

....

Optional further reflection

Listen to the song *No Greater Love* by Steven Curtis Chapman
(available on most streaming platforms).

Love's **trust**

'Having loved his own who were in the world, he loved them to the end.' (v1)

Some years ago I was visiting a church that I had never been to before, and at the end of the service they announced a time of foot-washing. I had never experienced this being practised in a church service before. I have to say my instinctive reaction towards it was mostly negative at first – mostly to do with personal embarrassment. I have always been a very independent person, and this seemed so strange to me.

A few years ago I had to have major surgery, and I was very, very scared. When I examined my feelings, I knew I was not afraid of dying. That was sure. I also knew I was not afraid of the surgery or pain specifically. So, I wondered, what was I so afraid of? When I finally worked it out, I realised that what I was really afraid of was losing my independence. I didn't want to have to ask for help. I wanted to be able to be in control. I think I understand how Peter felt that day when he objected to Jesus washing his feet. I also realised that was my problem with the foot-washing service too – I would have to let someone else minister to me. I would have to lay down my independence and allow myself to be vulnerable, at least for a while.

While I believe that washing His disciples' feet was an act of love on Jesus' part, I also think there is a message for us here (especially for independent people like me!). Jesus wants us to lay aside our independence and depend on Him. He wants closeness with us. He wants to feel our hurts with us and share our joys. Laying down our own desire for independence, becoming a part of each other – isn't that what loving a person is all about?

For prayer and reflection

Lord Jesus, help me to lay aside my independence and learn to be vulnerable with others. I want to serve people with the same heart You did. Amen.

Love **passed on**

Romans 12:3–10

'Be devoted to one another in love. Honour one another above yourselves.' (v10)

Are you familiar with the concept of paying something forward, instead of paying someone back? The basic idea is that instead of returning a favour to the person who helped you in the first place, you 'pay it forward' to someone else in need – and instead of expecting them to pay you back, they'll go on to bless someone else. In light of these verses from Romans, I'd like to challenge us today to reflect on the year ahead and resolve to be more loving to one another. How can we serve others above ourselves? Who can we include? How can we affirm and encourage those around us? Could we choose to value a relationship more than our need to be right about something?

It's easy to make positive resolutions now, but what about when we need extra help? The writer of the book of Hebrews tells us to 'approach God's throne of grace with confidence, so that we may receive mercy and find grace to help us in our time of need' (Heb. 4:16).

Sometimes we need a little extra dose of grace to deal with a situation, perhaps with a coworker or a family member, but learning to put that into action is key in learning to be more loving with other people.

Our reading today from Romans 12 shows us how everyone is important. In a church family, we all need to learn to get along. If you're finding this particularly difficult with someone, ask God to remind you of their enormous value to Him. We will never meet anyone on this earth who isn't utterly adored by God. Let's carry that wonderful fact with us into a new year, and pay it forward to everyone we encounter.

For prayer and reflection

Heavenly Father, please help me to be more like Jesus in this coming year. Help me to love more like He loved, even when I find it hard to do. Amen.